TECHNIQUES AND EQUIPMENT FOR WILDERNESS HORSE TRAVEL

U.S. Forest Service

**Fredonia Books
Amsterdam, The Netherlands**

Techniques and Equipment for Wilderness Horse Travel

by
U.S. Forest Service

ISBN: 1-4101-0817-1

Copyright © 2005 by Fredonia Books

Reprinted from the 1981 edition

Fredonia Books
Amsterdam, The Netherlands
http://www.fredoniabooks.com

All rights reserved, including the right to reproduce
this book, or portions thereof, in any form.

TECHNIQUES AND EQUIPMENT FOR WILDERNESS HORSE TRAVEL

ACKNOWLEDGMENTS

We want to thank the many horsemen who donated their ideas and time to the staff of the Missoula Equipment Development Center during the preparation of this text. Special thanks go to the Bitterroot Backcountry Horsemen, Montana Outfitters and Guides Association, Missoula Backcountry Horsemen, Wyoming Outfitters and Guides Association, Idaho Outfitters and Guides Association, American Horse Council, Washington State Horsemen, Trail Riders Association International, Ltd., North American Outfitters, and Montana Department of Fish, Wildlife and Parks for their ideas and critical comments. We particularly wish to thank Greg Risdahl, Missoula, Mont., who illustrated this booklet.

The use of trade, firm, or corporation names is for the information and convenience of the reader. Such use does not constitute an official evaluation, conclusion, recommendation, endorsement, or approval of any product or service to the exclusion of others that may be suitable.

PREFACE

Increasing numbers of visitors to wilderness have caused resource managers to seek information on good horse-handling techniques and innovative equipment to insure that "the benefits of an enduring resource of wilderness" are preserved.

This booklet is for those who travel into wilderness by horseback and who are concerned with minimizing man's impact there. Proper stock-handling, lightweight equipment, and good camp etiquette can do much to protect and preserve wilderness.

This booklet illustrates how light, compact gear can be used in the horse camp and emphasizes innovative horse equipment for more comfortable, convenient travel with pack stock. It contains equipment ideas and techniques for "minimum impact" wilderness travel developed over many years by outfitters, packers, horse groups, Forest Service personnel, and other horsemen. The appendixes give detailed information on equipment mentioned in the text.

CONTENTS

Techniques and Equipment for
Wilderness Horse Travel.................. 1

Appendixes
    A. Equipment List..................... 25

    B. Ridge Pole and Case 31

    C. Nose Bag......................... 37

    D. Picket-Pin 39

    E. Tree-Saver Strap 41

TECHNIQUES AND EQUIPMENT FOR WILDERNESS HORSE TRAVEL

America's wilderness trails are busier than ever before. Crowding, litter, pollution are becoming part of our wilderness experience. When wilderness visitors concentrate in the same areas, vegetation, soil, and water have little chance to recover. The result is bare ground, trampled roots, and polluted waters.

We face a choice as wilderness travelers: do nothing and see the quality of our wilderness experience decline, or reduce our impact on the land and see its beauty and solitude preserved.

The choice is obvious. We can reduce our impact and have a quality wilderness experience by keeping groups small, traveling the less-used trails, improving our camp etiquette, using lightweight and compact equipment, adopting a pack-it-in—pack-it-out philosophy, and striving for minimum impact.

Hikers have an incentive to lighten their packs. Recent advances in backpacking equipment make their choices almost unlimited, but what about those who travel horseback?

New, lighter, compact gear has a place in the horse camp. It saves time and trouble and reduces impact.

Outfitters, backcountry horsemen, and others have developed some ingenious techniques and equipment to reduce their impact and save their time. This booklet presents some of those ideas and what they can mean for wilderness travel with pack and saddle stock.

Your wilderness trip begins long before you arrive at the trail head. It starts with planning, preparing equipment, matching stock to the terrain you plan to travel, considering the weather, obtaining visitor permits and campfire permits where needed, and a host of other details.

For the old hands at going light, it means running through a well-worn check list.

Thanks to advances in lightweight gear, their camp is free of the heavy bulky equipment traditionally associated with horsepacking. Fewer stock are needed to pack their outfit. This means less impact.

Their equipment includes compact down or polyester filled sleeping bags. Lightweight foam sleeping pads or air mattresses are lighter and easier to pack than cots.

Even the canvas wall tent has its modern counterpart made of Camper Cloth. Camper Cloth is a waterproof cotton fabric half the weight of canvas.

Light aluminum ridgepoles and uprights break down for easy packing. And they assemble quickly.

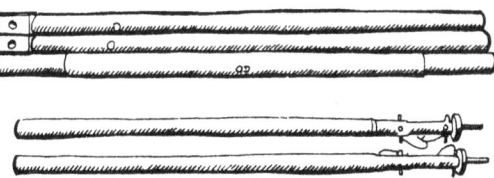

The two-person nylon A-frame tent is compact and weighs only a few pounds.

Lightweight nesting cookware and utensils reduce bulk and weight.

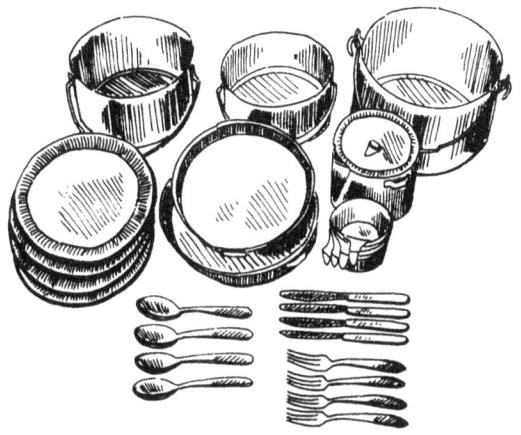

Campstoves ease the cooking chore and eliminate the need for cook fires.

Dehydrated foods are light and take up less space than canned goods. They are easy to prepare and reduce the garbage to be packed out.

To further cut down, the contents of glass jars and bottles are put into light plastic containers.

Instead of farrier tools and extra iron shoes, a lightweight urethane Easyboot serves as a spare, or protection for an injured hoof. A tool for tightening or pulling loose shoes and a rasp for trimming hooves are included.

 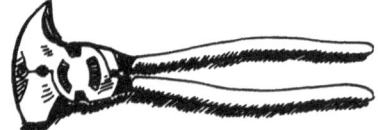 

Once all the gear is assembled, it's time to pack up. Manta tarps and panniers are commonly used.

Any item that can serve a number of purposes is desirable. Mantas are useful around camp as ground cloths, covers for tack, and emergency horse blankets.

Panniers allow easy access to gear on the trail and are handy for storage at camp.

For short trips, adequate gear and food can be carried in a cantle pack. Pommel pockets can be added to carry equipment on the front of the saddle.

Polypropylene rope is lighter and more durable than hemp for tying mantas and diamond hitches. Later it is used as a hitch line near camp.

Large panniers that fit over a riding saddle are convenient for those who don't mind walking in, but like a saddle for side trips from camp.

Animals conditioned to strenuous mountain travel are at home on the trail and accustomed to supplemental feeds and various methods of containment.

Supplemental feeds—hay and grain pellets and alfalfa cubes—can be a complete ration or combined with grazing. Waste is minimal and bulky hay bales are not needed.

Horses that react to strange looking ropes or corrals can cause damage or injure themselves. Introducing stock to hobbles, picket ropes, hitch lines, and various temporary corrals in a familiar environment may avert a major calamity at some remote camp.

Horses are trained to respect electric fence by leading them to it to be shocked once or twice before being left unattended.

Hemp or cotton is best for picket ropes and lead ropes because plastic rope can severely burn hide or skin and damage tree bark. A picket-pin that can be moved easily is desirable.

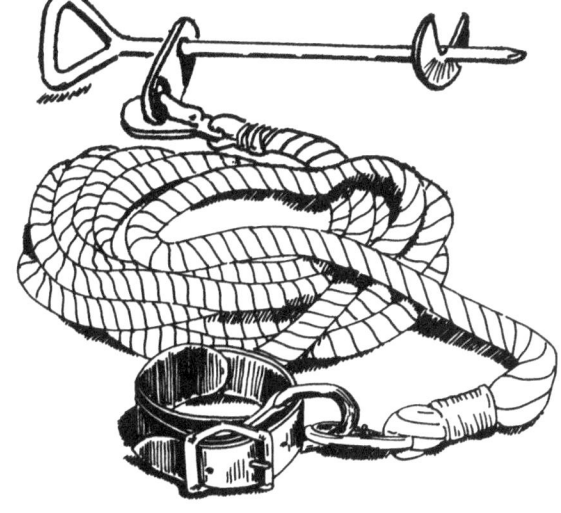

Animals correctly shod and properly packed stand quieter and cause less wear and tear on the trail than uncomfortable stock.

Once on the trail, care is taken to keep all stock single file. Multiple trails are prevented when stock are kept on one trail. Extra care is taken on open ridges and mountain meadows. Riders watch trail conditions and hold their horses from skirting shallow puddles and minor obstacles. Otherwise, wide deteriorated trails result.

On switchbacks, riders keep to the trail. Shortcutting switchbacks saves a few steps but quickly kills plant cover that prevents soil erosion. Erosion can destroy a trail.

At rest stops—even short ones—stock are tied well off the trail. It's courteous and minimizes trail wear. If it's a scenic overlook, historic site, or other popular stop, stock are kept out of the area.

A hitch line is a good idea. Stock can be quickly tied, kept in order, and easily watched.

Wide nylon "tree-saver straps" with quick-adjusting buckles are used for speed and convenience.

Rope is run between the straps, tied with a quick-release knot, and pulled taut.

Manure is always scattered after animals have been contained.

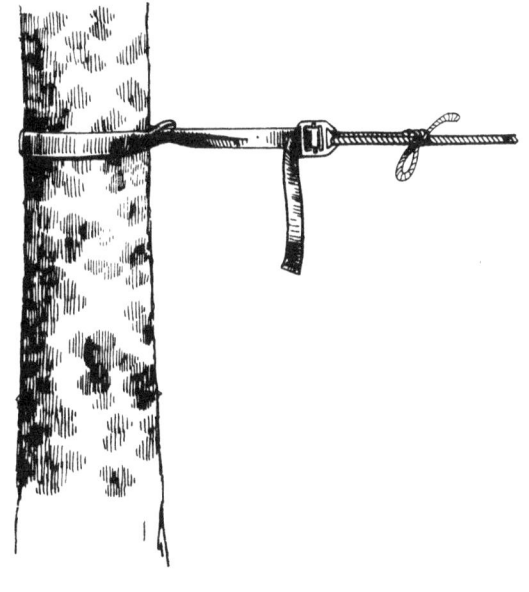

Trail obstacles are part of any wilderness journey. When possible riders clear trails to make travel easier for themselves and others. An ax or lightweight bow saw or crosscut saw can help remove most blowdown. When a detour is necessary, local managers are notified so the trail can be cleared before an alternate route forms.

At the end of a day on the trail, travelers need to look for a comfortable camp spot. They have a wider choice when they carry their own horse feed. Checking with local managers on forage conditions before a trip insures finding needed grazing.

Picking campsites that can withstand the impact of horses and people and don't have to be cleared of vegetation reduces damage. Durable sites, secluded from trails and other campers, and set back from creeks and shorelines, are best. Such spots get less use, and the woods offer protection from wind and sun.

Durability varies from season to season. A campsite in early spring may contain young, easily damaged vegetation and moist soils. But the same site in summer may have hardy vegetation and dry soils. High alpine meadows are fragile anytime.

Stock are never kept in camp. They are tied some distance away. The hitch line with tree-saver straps goes up first.

Later a pole can also be tied between two trees to form a hitch rail.

Animals familiar with one another are left to graze with only a wrangle horse picketed. His picket-pin is moved often to prevent overgrazing. The other animals will remain close by. Some may need to be hobbled.

A temporary corral is a good idea for parties camping several days at one spot. They have three choices: poles, rope, or electric fence.

A pole corral is practical where pole-size deadfall is abundant.

Poles are secured with rope using wood shims or gunny sacks to protect the bark. This method doesn't damage trees like wire or nails. Some intermediate posts, cut from downfall, may need to be set when trees are far apart.

A rope corral is not as secure as a pole corral. But it is easier to erect and remove. And it doesn't need native poles. One method uses two parallel ropes tied with frequent loops or bowlines so cross ropes can be threaded through to make a more secure enclosure.

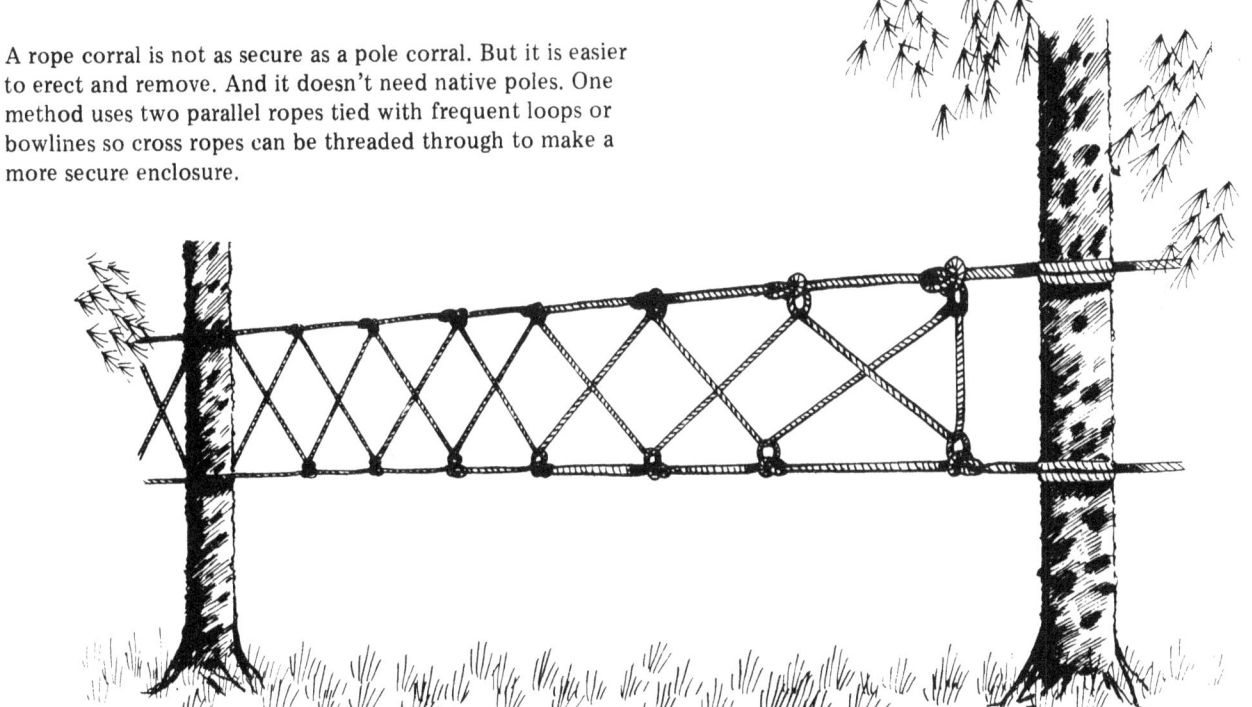

Once stock are trained to respect electric fence, it may be the most convenient temporary corral or pasture. Several new electric fence systems are lightweight and easily and quickly put up and moved.

One system uses a 3½-pound solid-state fence charger that requires only six flashlight batteries, lightweight plastic posts, and aluminized plastic ribbon called Glo-Gard instead of steel wire. It requires no native materials and makes a secure enclosure. The Glo-Gard and plastic posts needed to enclose ½ acre of pasture weigh only 18 pounds.

Some combination of rope and poles and electric fence may be the best solution when one type alone is impractical.

Where a hitch rail, hitch line, picket, or corral is not feasible, and stock must be tied to trees for more than short periods, only mature trees are used. Ropes are tied securely to prevent slippage. Soft, thick ropes are easier on bark and so is a double-wrapped hitch.

Hobbling greatly reduces damage to tree roots.

Flies and mosquitos aggravate stock, making them very restless when tied.

Bug repellent and fringed eye guards ease their torment so they stand quieter.

Stock are led to water at a rocky spot where little bank damage will occur. Soft or marshy lake edges are avoided

Water can be carried to stock in a light collapsible bucket that also serves for drowning fires and hauling wash water.

Supplemental feeds in cubes and pellets can be fed on the ground or preferably in nose bags.

A pellet ration may not supply the bulk that makes a horse feel full. Animals become restless and chew ropes and poles and strip bark from trees. A few hours of grazing or feeding smaller rations more often helps stop such behavior.

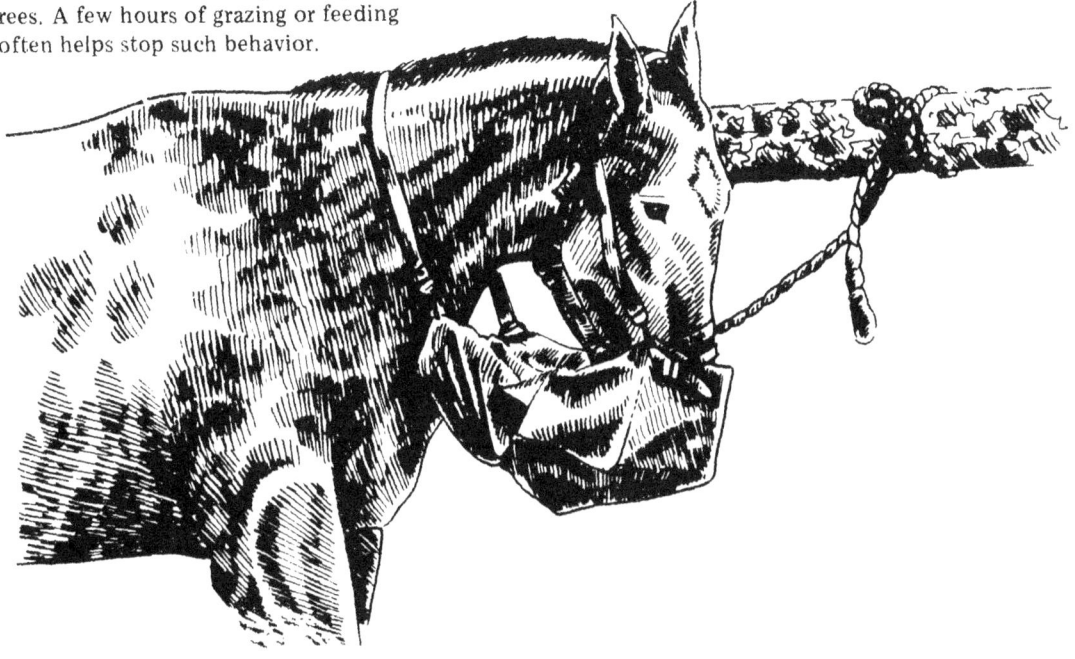

Most pellets contain enough salt to satisfy stock for a few days. But for long trips, animals need additional salt. Only salt blocks are used. They are set out in a notched log or other container. This prevents rain from leaching salt into the soil, destroying vegetation, and attracting wildlife that paw up the ground. Unused salt is packed out.

During the camp stay, every effort is made to keep man's impact small. Care is taken not to contaminate water sources with stock or human waste. Washing chores are done with biodegradable soaps. Waste water is dumped well away from water sources. Human waste is buried in the biotic layer of the soil.

Fires are kept small and only dead and down wood is burned. Existing fire rings are used. Otherwise a suitable fire pit is dug and the dirt and sod saved. Grass close to the edge is trimmed back.

Food scraps, bits of paper, and bacon grease can be burned. Everything else is packed out. Burying garbage or burning aluminum foil is no longer an acceptable disposal method.

And when it's time to break camp nothing is left behind. All unburned refuse is packed up. Burned out cans from the fire pit are crushed for easy packing.

Temporary hitch rails and corrals are dismantled, and manure piles are scattered to aid decomposition, discourage flies, and as a courtesy to others.

Large objects cleared from the area are put back in place. Ropes are removed from trees.

The fire is drowned dead out, unused fire wood is scattered, fire rings are dismantled, and the fire pit is filled in with the original dirt and sod. The camp is returned to its normal state.

Wilderness visits widely scattered in time and space cause little impact. But concentrated in the same areas, the land has little chance to recover. Adopting techniques and equipment to minimize our impact, then seeking out the less-crowded country, will help insure that future wilderness visits are in unspoiled beauty and solitude.

APPENDIX A
Equipment List

Equipment Item	Description of Materials	Weight	Brand Names	Some Sources[*]	Cost	Comments
1. Sleeping bags	Rip-stop nylon outer and inner shell; down or polyester (Polar Guard or Dacron Hollofil II) fill insulation.	3 lb 8 oz to 5 lb	(a) Eastern Mountain Sports, Inc. (EMS) (b) Recreational Equip., Inc. (REI) (c) Slumberjack (d) The North Face (e) White Stag (f) Sierra Designs	(a) Eastern Mountain Sports, Inc. (b) Recreational Equip., Inc. (c) Local sporting goods stores (d) The North Face; local sporting goods stores; Eastern Mountain Sports, Inc.; Don Gleason's Campers Supply, Inc. (e) Local sporting goods stores (f) Sierra Designs; local sporting goods stores	$50 to $150	Down gives the most warmth and compression for weight. Rip-stop nylon is down proof and strong for its weight (1.5 oz to 1.9 oz per sq yd fabric is usually used). Down is expensive. Polyester fiber insulation is much cheaper, works fine, and is warm when wet because it won't clump like wet down. A taper bag design, by eliminating extraneous material, is more compactable, lightweight, and more heat efficient than a rectangular bag.
2. Foam sleeping pads	Open-cell polyurethane foam for padding. Outer covering of waterproof nylon fabric (bottom), and nonslip cotton/polyester (top). Usually two sizes: about 22" x 48" and 22" x 72".	1 lb 4 oz to 2 lb	(a) EMS (b) REI (c) Sierra Designs (d) The North Face (e) Don Gleasons	(a) Eastern Mountain Sports, Inc. (b) Recreational Equip., Inc. (c) Sierra Designs; local sporting goods stores (d) The North Face; local sporting goods stores (e) Don Gleason's Campers Supply, Inc.	$10 to $18	Provides good cushion and insulation for sleeping. They are lightweight and reasonably compressible. Don't have to be blown up like an air mattress and can't puncture.
3. Air mattresses	New ultralightweight air mattresses are very compact and easy to blow up because they use tubes with individual valves. If one tube punctures, others remain intact. They use coated nylon fabrics. Usually two sizes: deflated they measure about 28" x 44" and 28" x 72".	7 oz to 12 oz	(a) Stebco (b) Hampshire	(a) Eastern Mountain Sports, Inc.; local sporting goods stores (b) Don Gleason's Campers Supply, Inc.; Recreational Equip., Inc.; local sporting goods stores.	$16 to $23	Provides good cushion but limited insulation. Very lightweight and compact.
	Standard air mattresses are usually larger and heavier than the above types. Coated nylon fabrics are the most durable. Usual sizes are about 24" x 50" and 26" to 30" x 72" to 76" deflated.	2 lb to 6 lb	(a) White Stag (b) Stebco	(a) Local sporting goods stores; Don Gleason's Campers Supply, Inc. (b) Local sporting goods stores; Don Gleason's Campers Supply, Inc.	$12 to $25	Heavier and bulkier than the new ultralights.

Equipment Item	Description of Materials	Weight	Brand Names	Some Sources*	Cost	Comments
4. Combination air/foam mattresses	1"-thick open cell foam sealed inside; durable nylon fabric air mattress. Expands to 1½" thick when allowed to inflate (somewhat self-inflating) but compacts very well when deflated and rolled tightly.	1 lb 8 oz (19" x 48") 2 lb 5 oz (19" x 72")	Therm-A-Rest	Local sporting goods stores; Eastern Mountain Sports; Recreational Equip., Inc.; Don Gleason's Campers Supply, Inc.	$ 35 (19" x 48") $ 50 (19" x 72")	Offers advantages over both foam pads and air mattresses, but is more expensive. The combination mattress uses air for extra cushion while foam minimizes body heat loss. They roll up compactly because air in foam escapes through valve. Mattress is somewhat self-inflating because foam expands as air returns through opened valve (they usually need to be further inflated by mouth).
5. "Camper Cloth" wall tents	"Camper Cloth" is an extra high count drill finished with a dry, water repellent, mildew-resistant treatment; it is light tan in color and weighs 8.53 oz per sq yd. Various tent sizes are available.	a 10' x 10' tent with 4' wall weighs 22 lb	Colorado Tent Co.	Colorado Tent Co.	$150 to $250	For those who like the roominess of a wall tent, this company offers a good selection of sizes and options. The lightweight, tightly woven cotton "Camper Cloth" is durable and waterproof without the need for extra waterproof treatments required by tents of cotton duck; and about half the weight.
6. Two-person nylon tents	Usually variations of the A-frame style with about 5' x 7' of floor space. Best designs have breathable inner tent and an outer waterproof fly. Inner Tent—Uncoated rip-stop nylon upper; coated taffeta nylon floor. Floor extends up side walls about 12". End panels same as floor. Outerfly—Coated rip-stop nylon. (Tents of Gortex fabric, which breaths and is yet 100% waterproof, require only one layer of Gortex throughout— except that coated taffeta is used for the floor.)	5 lb 8 oz to 7 lb 8 oz	(a) EMS (b) REI (c) Eureka (d) The North Face (e) Sierra Designs (f) White Stag	(a) Eastern Mountain Sports, Inc. (b) Recreational Equip., Inc. (c) Eureka Tent Inc.; local sporting goods stores; Eastern Mountain Sports, Inc.; Don Gleason's Campers Supply, Inc. (d) The North Face; local sporting goods stores; Eastern Mountain Sports, Inc.; Don Gleason's Campers Supply, Inc. (e) Sierra Designs; local sporting goods stores (f) Local sporting goods stores; Don Gleason's Campers Supply, Inc.	$ 90 to $250	More confining than wall tents but easy to put up. Nylon fabric must be coated with a thin film of plastic to make it waterproof. Tents made entirely of coated nylon cannot breathe. Moisture inside the tent condenses on the walls and drips. Nylon tents that have an inner breathable tent and an outer waterproof rain fly are best. The new Gortex tents are lighter than a two-layer tent but are much more expensive. A-frame tents have been popular because they are sturdy and lightweight. Recently, many new tent designs have come out such as domes and variations of the dome. They have some advantages over the A-frame, such as more interior space, but cost much more. A-frame and dome-shaped tents are available in 3- and 4-person sizes as well as the standard 2-person size.
7. Aluminum ridge poles and uprights	Adjustable lightweight poles for supporting tents cooking flys, lean-tos, etc. Tempered aluminum tubing is best.	Poles for a 10' x 10' wall tent weigh 6 lb	(a) White Stag (b) REI (c) MEDC drawing	(a) Local sporting goods stores (may have to be special ordered from distributor) (b) Recreational Equip., Inc. (c) See appendix B	$ 12 to $ 20	Aluminum poles are strong, lightweight, and collapsible. Standard with 2-person A-frame style or dome tents but optional on most wall tents. Self-supporting tents eliminate need to gather tent poles at camp sites or tie ridge lines to trees.
8. Cookware and utensils	Aluminum cooking pots and pans. Plastic or aluminum plates, cups, bowls etc.			Local sporting goods stores; Eastern Mountain Sports; Recreational Equip., Inc.; Don Gleason's Campers Supply, Inc.		Aluminum ware is lighter than steel or cast iron cookware, heats quickly, but does not hold heat as well as the other two kinds. Nesting aluminum pots and pans take up less space. Square pots and pans seem to pack better than round shapes.

Equipment Item	Description of Materials	Weight	Brand Names	Some Sources*	Cost	Comments
9. Stoves	Portable, single- or double-burner gasoline or propane stoves.	11 oz to 11 lb	(a) Coleman (b) Svea (c) Optimus (d) MSR (e) Gaz (f) Primus	(a-f) Local sporting goods stores; Eastern Mountain Sports; Recreational Equip., Inc.; Don Gleason's Campers Supply, Inc.; Mountain Safety Research, Inc.	$15 to $60	Portable liquid fuel stoves are convenient, lightweight, and eliminate the need to gather firewood. Small stoves greatly simplify the chore of cooking food outdoors. White gasoline is cheaper to use than pressurized canister of propane or butane. Disposable fuel canisters also present a potential garbage problem.
10. Freeze-dried foods	Freeze-dried or other dehydrated foods.	2 lb per person per day	(a) Mountain House (Oregon Freeze-Dry) (b) Rich Moor (c) Dri-Lite (d) EMS	(a-c) Don Gleason's Campers Supply, Inc.; Recreational Equip., Inc.; Eastern Mountain Sports; local sporting goods stores and grocery stores (d) Eastern Mountain Sports		Freeze-dried foods are much lighter and less bulky than fresh or canned foods. There is no danger of spoilage and no refrigeration is needed. Most FD foods are precooked and require only a few minutes to reconstitute in hot water. FD foods are getting expensive but other cheaper dehydrates available as supermarket items can be used to build a meal around a FD entree. FD foods in bulk are cheaper.
11. Reusable plastic food containers	Reusable polyethylene, polypropeline, or polyvinyl food storage containers. Large and small mouth in various sizes.	2/3 oz to 2 oz		Local sporting goods stores; Eastern Mountain Sports; Recreational Equip., Inc.; Don Gleason's Campers Supply, Inc.	$.40 to $.75	Transferring foods from glass jars or cans to reusable plastic containers eliminates breakage, weight, and potential litter. Many good durable poly bottles are free for the asking from local pharmacists.
12. Fencing pliers		1 lb		Hardware stores; farm and ranch supply stores, etc.		Used for pulling or tightening loose horseshoes and for repairing equipment.
13. Rasp		1 lb 8 oz		Hardware stores; farm and ranch supply stores, etc.		Used for shaping hooves
14. Easyboot	Urathane plastic horseshoe fits over and around the hoof like a boot. It is tightened on and held in place by a cable and buckle system.	13 oz each	Easyboot	Les-Kare, Inc.; Miller Stockman; local saddle shops	$20 each or 4/$76	Can be used in place of normal iron shoes or can be carried as a spare shoe. Easy to install, but hooves need to be shaped for proper fit. Provides good traction on rock and ice and protects the hoof. Horses adapt quickly to use. Longer wearing than iron shoes. Handy for people who only make a few trips per year and don't want their horse shod just for that.
15. Mantas	Heavy canvas tarps. Usually 6' x 7' or 6' x 6'.	6 lb		Ray Holes Saddle Co.; Colorado Tent Co.; local canvas shops	$14 to $16	Usually used with the Decker pack saddle. Mantas allow a variety of odd-shaped items to be packed. Handy as ground cloths and other uses around camp.
16. Panniers	Heavy canvas, canvas and leather, or nylon pack bags. About 24" x 16" x 11". (Panniers are also often made of plywood, fiber glass, plastic, rawhide or aluminum.)	4 lb to 6 lb each	(a) Ray Holes (canvas and leather) (b) Pro outfitter (nylon, plastic) (c) Scatpac (plastic) (d) Colorado Tent Co. (canvas) (e) Colorado Saddlery (canvas)	(a) Ray Holes Saddle Co. (b) Morgan Horse Products (c) Ralide Corp., Inc. (d) Colorado Tent Co. (e) Colorado Saddlery Co.	$50 to $160 per pair	Easier to use than mantas but not as versatile for odd-sized items. Panniers are convenient to get into on the trail and are handy for storing items around camp. (Pack boxes made of wood, fiber glass, aluminum, or plastic are often used and just as handy.)

Equipment Item	Description of Materials	Weight	Brand Names	Some Sources*	Cost	Comments
17. Saddle packs (cantal packs)	Have 3-5 zippered compartments and are usually made of 8-oz waterproof nylon fabric. Fit behind saddle and extend down over horse's flanks. About 48" x 16" x 9".	2 lb	(a) Sheplers own (b) Morgan's super Pack (c) Gerry Horse Pac (d) Saddlepak	(a) Shepler, Inc. (b) Morgan Horse Products (c) Local saddle shops (d) Regis Co.	$ 35 to $ 75	This pack can carry enough food and lightweight gear for weekend trips, rides well on a horse, and is convenient to use. Pack should have soft items next to horse and not be overloaded.
18. Riding saddle panniers	Heavyweight canvas panniers that fit down over a riding saddle.	6 lb	Colorado Saddlery	Colorado Saddlery Co.; Miller Stockmen; local saddle shops	$ 77	These panniers eliminate the need for a pack animal if a horseman wishes to walk and lead horse to camp. Once there, saddle horse is available for rides out from camp. Hunters can use them for hauling out game.
19. Nose bags (feed bags)	Generally two types: (a) cylindrical shape about 8" x 12" (canvas or nylon) with single head strap; fits over horse's muzzle; (b) GI style designed by the U.S. Army for cavalry horses (flat canvas bag about 13" x 21" that fits under a horse's neck and around muzzle and uses a neck strap and a head strap. Can be made of nylon instead of canvas for lighter weight and low bulk).	2 lb	(a) Various brands (b) GI; MEDC drawing	(a) Local saddle shops; Morgan Horse Products; Sheplers, Inc.; Ray Holes Saddle Co.; Colorado Saddlery Co. (b) Army surplus stores; local saddle shops; see appendix C	$ 5 to $ 17	Nosebags eliminate waste when feeding pellets or grain. The GI type further reduces waste because horse cannot throw feed out when he throws his head. A day's ration can be folded inside this type and carried on the trail.
20. Hobbles	"Utah hobbles"—all-leather, twin loops. Other hobbles are of harness leather and connected with swivels and chain or all-leather figure 8 type.	1 lb to 1 lb 8 oz		Local saddle shops; Ray Holes Saddle Co.; Sheplers, Inc.; Morgan Horse Products; Colorado Saddlery Co.	$ 6 to $ 17	Hobbles can keep horses from straying too far from camp and from pawing the ground when they must be tied to trees. The Utah type hobble can be carried around a horse's neck for quick access when hobbling is needed.
21. Picket-hobble	Single leg hobble or "half-a-hobble" of the leather, chain, and swivel type.	8 oz		Local saddle shops; Morgan Horse Products; Colorado Saddlery Co.	$ 7	A picket hobble is used on one front foot and attached to a picket rope. A horse confined this way must be moved often to prevent overgrazing.
22. Picket-pin	Auger type (steel rod with auger disk at point or corkscrew shape) 16" - 18" long.	1 lb 8 oz	MEDC drawing	See appendix D	$ 5	A picket-pin eliminates the need to cut and pound in a wooden stake or picket to a log or small tree. It can also eliminate the tendency to let a picketed horse graze too long in one spot. The new lightweight auger-type steel pin is easy to carry, easy to place, and easy to move.
Manta ropes and sling ropes	Polypropylene or hemp.			Farm and ranch supply stores; hardware stores; saddle shops	$ .15 to $ .30 per foot	Polypropylene will not absorb water and freeze up like hemp rope and is lighter. Comes in various colors such as yellow for easy visibility. Generally, wears longer than hemp or cotton rope when used for tying mantas, etc. Nylon rope is strong, soft, and flexible and makes good pack ropes but is much more expensive than the other two kinds.
24. Lead ropes and picket ropes	Cotton or hemp.			Farm and ranch supply stores; hardware stores; saddle shops	$ 10	Is softer than plastic rope so less likely to cause rope burns to stock.

Equipment Item	Description of Materials	Weight	Brand Names	Some Sources*	Cost	Comments
25. Tree-saver straps	Wide nylon webbing (about 2" wide and 6' to 9' long) with adjustable self-locking v-buckle. Two tree-saver straps are used with rope to form a quick, adjustable hitch line between two trees.	8 oz each	MEDC drawing	See appendix E	$ 4 to $ 5 each	Used around trees so that a rope can be easily tied and tightened between two such straps to create a hitch line (also called a highline or picket line). The tree-saver strap protects the tree's bark from rope chafe and the self-locking buckle allows the rope to be easily pulled taut. A hitch line provides a place to tie horses so they are well away from tree roots that are easily damaged from trampling.
26. Electric fence	Portable electric fencing allows stock to be contained without the need for hobbles, picket ropes, pole corrals, or hitch lines. One of the newest and lightest fencing materials is called Glo-Gard and is made of 3/8"-wide aluminized plastic ribbon that conducts electricity and is highly visible. Other components include light-weight plastic posts (and drill for post holes), gate handles, ribbon holders for posts, and reel and crank.	Glo-Gard: 1 lb/328' of ribbon; posts, 8 oz each; reel and crank 2 lb 12 oz	Glo-Gard	International Equip., Inc.; farm and ranch supply stores		Glo-Gard is a nonmechanical electric fence system designed to virtually eliminate fence injuries to animals. It works on the principle of arousing the animals curiosity for the shiny ribbon and the aversion to it when shocked by it. All components are designed to bend or break if hit by an animal, removing many of the concerns about using steel wire fence in the back-country. A single strand of ribbon should be enough for horses or mules. The plastic posts are usually set about 15' apart. Glo-Gard is lightweight and easy to handle and can be installed in a fraction of the time of conventional fencing. It can be lowered, raised, or added to easily and quickly, and can be taken down and set up over and over, using the reel and crank. Repairs easily made with splicers and a pair of pliers. The ribbon can be attached to wooden or steel posts and to trees. When it is being installed it will twist naturally, forming many reflecting surfaces visible from any angle.
	Another new and very lightweight material is called Polywire. Six very fine strands of stainless wire are woven in with plastic strands to form a cord 1/16" in diameter.	14 oz/660'	Polywire	Farm and ranch supply stores; hardware stores; Live Wire Products	$10	The small strands of steel wire carry electrical current and plastic strands provide strength. Polywire can be attached to trees or wooden posts or poles with special screw-in type plastic insulators to create a versatile, lightweight, effective stock enclosure. It is also compatible with Glo-Gard components.
27. Fence charger	A solid-state model operates off 6 D-size flashlight batteries. It is 11" long and 3-1/2" in diameter, and is capable of 5,000 volts output and consistantly produces 3,000 to 4,500 volts. Will charge 1 to 3 miles of fence for 6 weeks on one set of batteries.	3 lb 11 oz with batteries	Speedrite Mk. V.	Live Wire Products	$80	This is the smallest, lightest fence charger available. It is very portable and can be used on any electric fence. Very compatible with Glo-Gard and Polywire.
28. Bug repellent	Fly, mosquito, and gnat repellents and insecticides.		(a) Wipe (b) Repel-x (c) Swat	(a-c) Farm and ranch supply stores; hardware stores; saddle shops; Colorado Saddlery Co.; Sheplers, Inc.	$ 6 to $ 9 per quart	Eases horses' torment from biting insects and allows them to stand quieter on the trail and at camp.

Equipment Item	Description of Materials	Weight	Brand Names	Some Sources[*]	Cost	Comments
29. Fringed eyeguards (fly net)	A 12" fringe is attached to the brow band of a headstall and secured with a throat latch so it hangs from horse's forehead to nose.	8 oz		Colorado Saddlery Co.	$10	Very good for controlling flies around eyes of horses and mules. Easy to put on. Stock stand quieter when not bothered by flies.
30. Collapsible bucket	Large capacity (16 qt) with wire rim, long adjustable nylon carrying strap, solid bottom, and heavy-duty, double-wall vinyl or reinforced vinyl construction.	1 lb 2 oz		Farm and ranch supply stores; local saddle shops; hardware stores	$5 to $10	Strong, lightweight, and collapsible. Handy for watering horses and carrying water for camp use. Long adjustable strap lets bucket double as a feed bag in a pinch.
31. Bell and collar	Leather strap collar and large metal cowbell.	1 lb 8 oz		Local saddle shops; hardware stores; Sheplers, Inc.; Colorado Saddlery Co.	$6 to $7	When stock are turned out to graze, at least one horse is belled so that their movements can be monitored. Large noisy bells are best because stock can stray far from camp.

*Complete Names, Addresses, and Telephone Numbers of Equipment Sources

Colorado Saddlery Co.
1631 15th St.
Denver, CO 80202
(303) 572-8350

Colorado Tent Co.
2228 Blake
Denver, CO 80216
(303) 825-3855

Don Gleason's Campers Supply, Inc.
P.O. Box 87
Northampton, MA 01060
(413) 584-4895

Eastern Mountain Sports
Two Vose Farm Rd.
Peterborough, NH 03458
(603) 924-9212

Eureka Tent, Inc.
625 Conklin Rd.
P.O. Box 966
Binghamton, NY 13902
(607) 723-7546

International Equipment, Inc.
P.O. Box 652
Woodinville, WA 98072
(206) 827-5402

Les-Kare, Inc.
P.O. Box AAA
Pojoaque, NM 87501
(505) 455-7817

Live Wire Products
P.O. Box 150
Grass Valley, CA 95945
(916) 273-9397

Miller Stockman
P.O. Box 5407
Denver, CO 80217
(303) 429-6578

Morgan Horse Products
P.O. Box 100
Ellsworth, NE 69340
(308) 762-4884

Mountain Safety Research, Inc.
South 96th St. at Eighth Ave. South
Seattle, WA 98108
(206) 762-0210

The North Face
1234 Fifth St.
Berkeley, CA 94710
(415) 548-1371

Ralide Corp., Inc.
P.O. Box 131
Athens, TN 37303
(615) 745-3524

Ray Holes Saddle Co.
Grangeville, ID 83530
(208) 983-1460

Recreational Equipment, Inc.
1525 11th Ave.
Seattle, WA 98122
(800) 426-4840

Regis Co.
P.O. Box 726
Lake Mary, FL 32746

Sheplers, Inc.
P.O. Box 7702
Wichita, KA 67277
(316) 942-8211

Sierra Designs
247 Fourth St.
Berkeley, CA 94607
(800) 227-1120

Slumberjack, Inc.
P.O. Box 31405
Los Angeles, CA 90031

MATERIALS LIST

NO	PART NAME	REQD	MATERIAL—DESCRIPTION
1	END SECTION*	2	PARTS 4, 5, & 7
2	MID SECTION*	3	PARTS 4, 6, 7, & 8
3	CONNECTOR*	1	PARTS 4, 6, 7, & 8
4	TUBE	6	2" SCH 40 ALUM PIPE
5	END	2	2" DIA HIGH DENSITY POLYETHELENE
6	JOINT	4	2" OD X .065 WALL STEEL TUBE
7	FASTENERS	20	1/4" DIA X 1/4 GRIP BRAZIER HEAD HAMMER DRIVEN BLIND RIVET
8	END PLUG	5	16 GA STEEL SHEET

*These are the number of sections for a 16-foot tent. For tents of other lengths, the number of midsections will vary and connector length will increase from 6 inches.

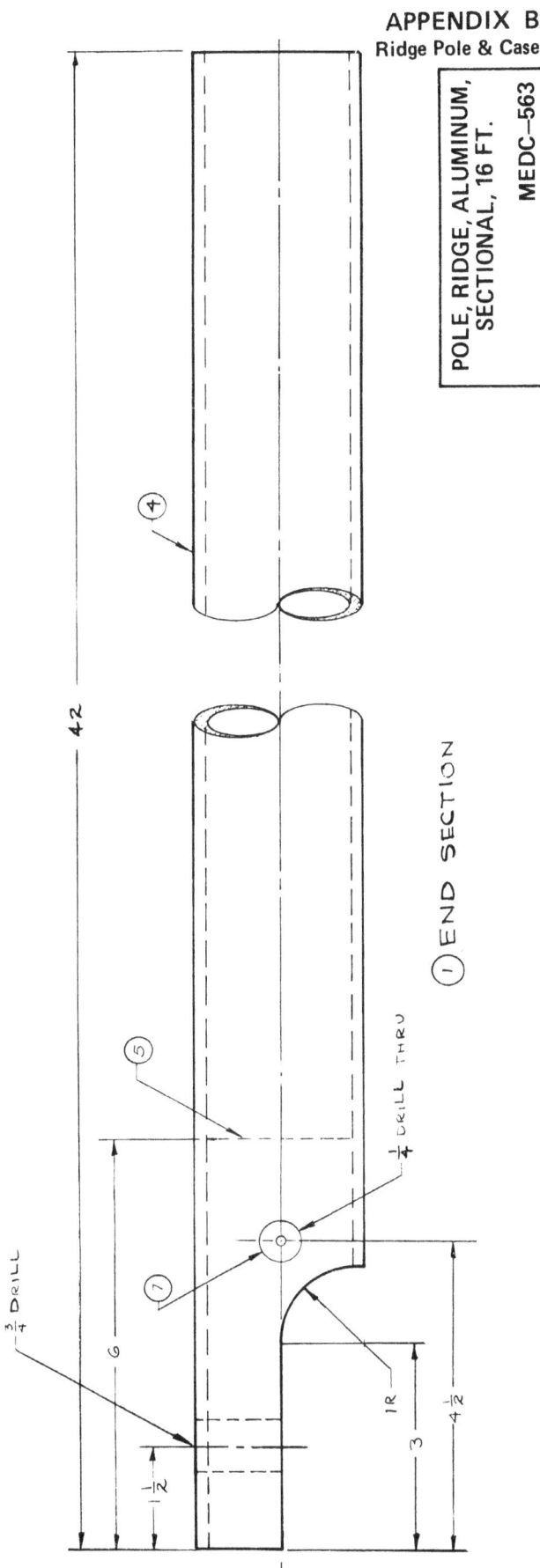

APPENDIX B
Ridge Pole & Case

POLE, RIDGE, ALUMINUM, SECTIONAL, 16 FT.

MEDC–563

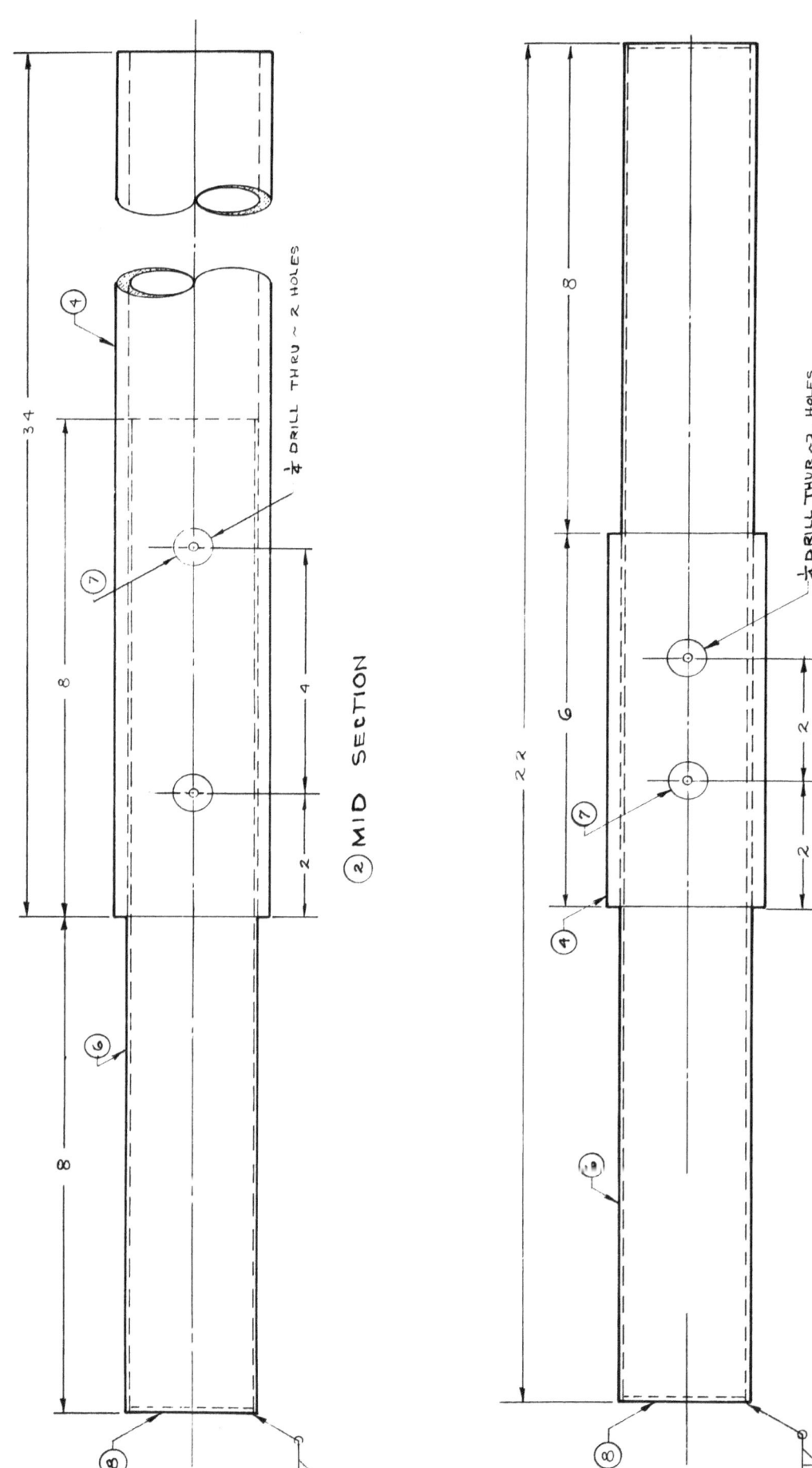

MATERIALS LIST

NO	PART NAME	REQD	MATERIAL DESCRIPTION	SHEET
1	MAIN PANEL	2	CLOTH, DUCK, COTTON, NO. 6 TYPE I OF CCC-C-419, COLOR AND TREATMENT SHALL BE TYPE I, CLASS B OF CCC-D-950, OD NO 7	
2	BOTTOM	4		
3	WEBBING	AS REQD	COTTON, 1-INCH WIDTH, TYPE IIb, CLASS 4 OF MIL-W-530, OD NO 7	
4	THREAD	AS REQD	POLYESTER, TYPE I, CLASS I, SHADE S-1 OF V-T-285, SIZE FF	
5	BUCKLE	4	TONGUELESS, 2-BAR, TYPE II, STYLE 1, CLASS 1, SIZE 1-INCH OF MIL-B-543	
6	END CLIP	4	BALL END CLIP, TYPE I, CLASS 1, SIZE 1-INCH OF MIL-C-496	

NOTES:
1. STITCHING - ALL STITCHING SHALL BE TYPE 301 OF FED STD NO 751, 6 TO 8 STITCHES PER INCH.

2. THREAD BREAKS - SHALL BE OVERSTITCHED NOT LESS THAN 1-INCH AT EACH BREAK.

3. STITCHING ENDS - ENDS OF ALL STITCHING SHALL BE OVERSTITCHED OR TURNED UNDER IN A HEM OR HELD BY OTHER STITCHING.

4. SETTING OF END CLIP - WEBBING SHALL BE INSERTED THE FULL DEPTH OF THE CLIP. CLIPS SHALL BE SECURELY SET WITHOUT CUTTING THE WEBBING AND THE WEBBING SHALL LIE FLAT AT THE CLIP.

5. WORKMANSHIP - CLOTH SHALL BE FREE OF HOLES, CUTS AND TEARS. WEBBINGS SHALL NOT HAVE SCALLOPED EDGES. THREAD TENSION SHALL BE MAINTAINED SO THERE WILL BE NO LOOSE STITCHING. TAKE CARE NOT TO INCUR NEEDLE CHEWS IN SEWING. TRIM ALL THREAD ENDS TO 1/2 INCH OR LESS. METAL COMPONENTS SHALL BE FREE OF BURRS, SHARP EDGES AND SHALL NOT BE BROKEN OR MALFORMED.

6. MARKING - IDENTIFICATION MARKING SHALL BE APPLIED AS SHOWN WITH A BLACK PAINT OR INK WHICH IS WATER RESISTANT.

UNLESS OTHERWISE SPECIFIED
TOLERANCES SHALL BE AS FOLLOWS:
LESS THAN 2 INCHES ± 1/16
2 TO 10 INCHES   ± 1/8
OVER 10 INCHES   ± 1/4

CASE, TENT POLES

MEDC - 463

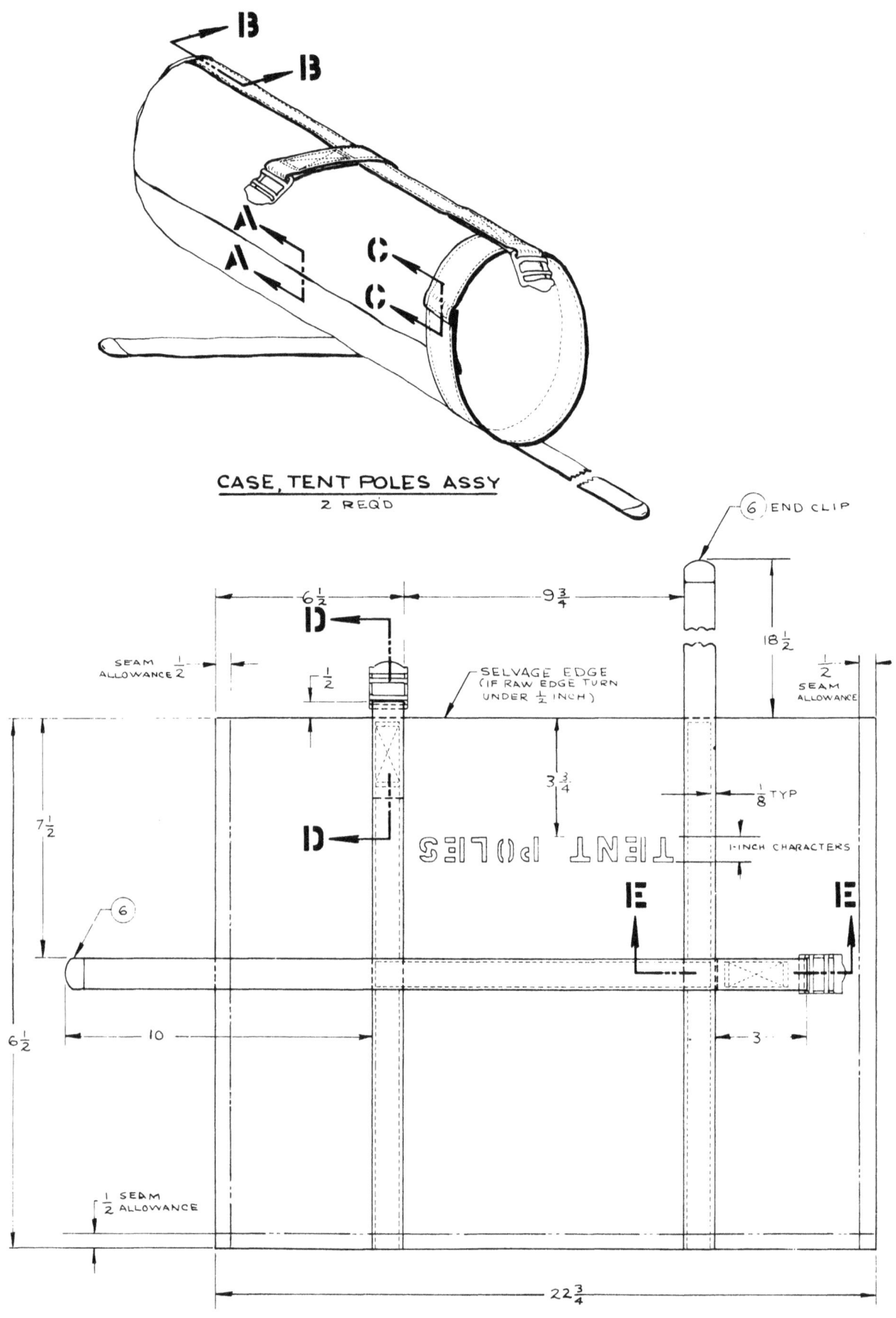

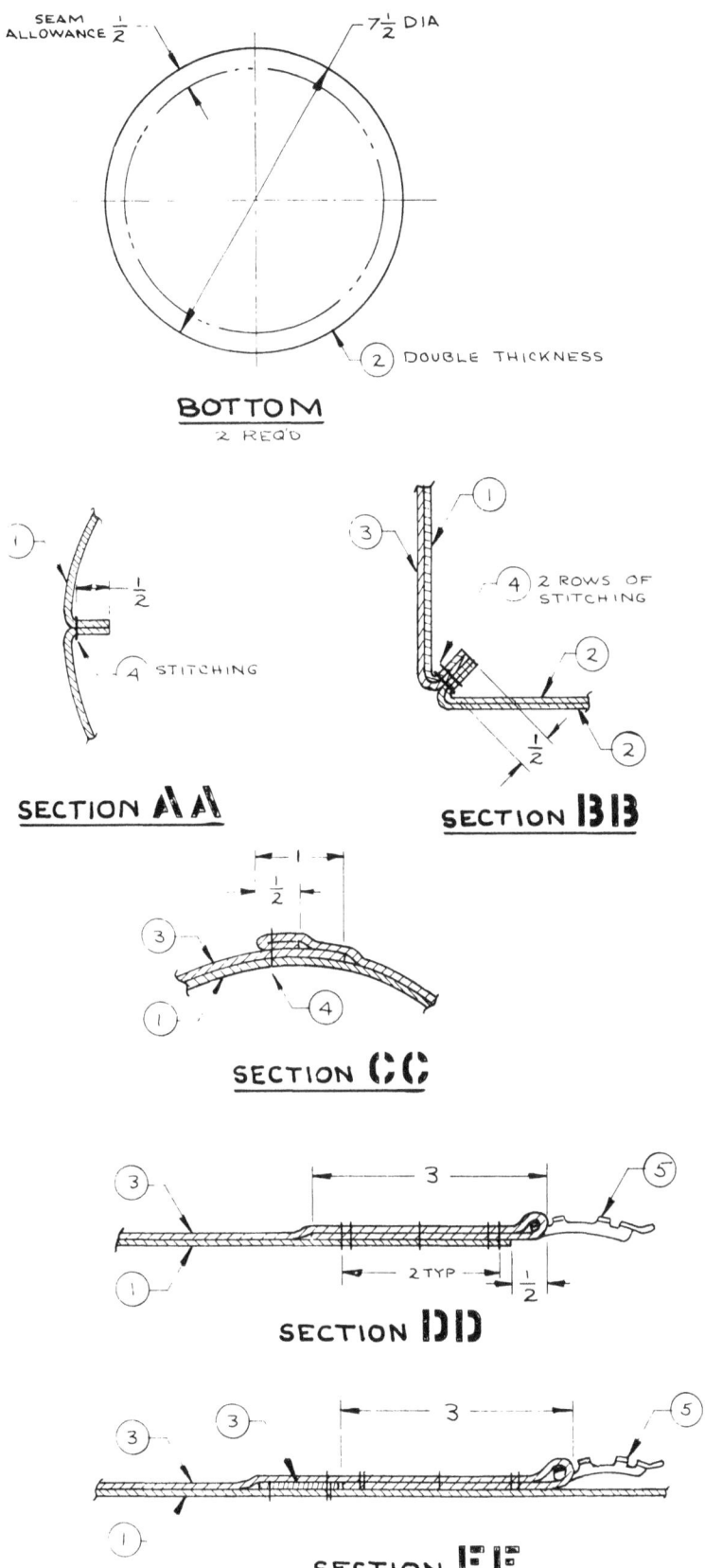

APPENDIX C
Nose Bag

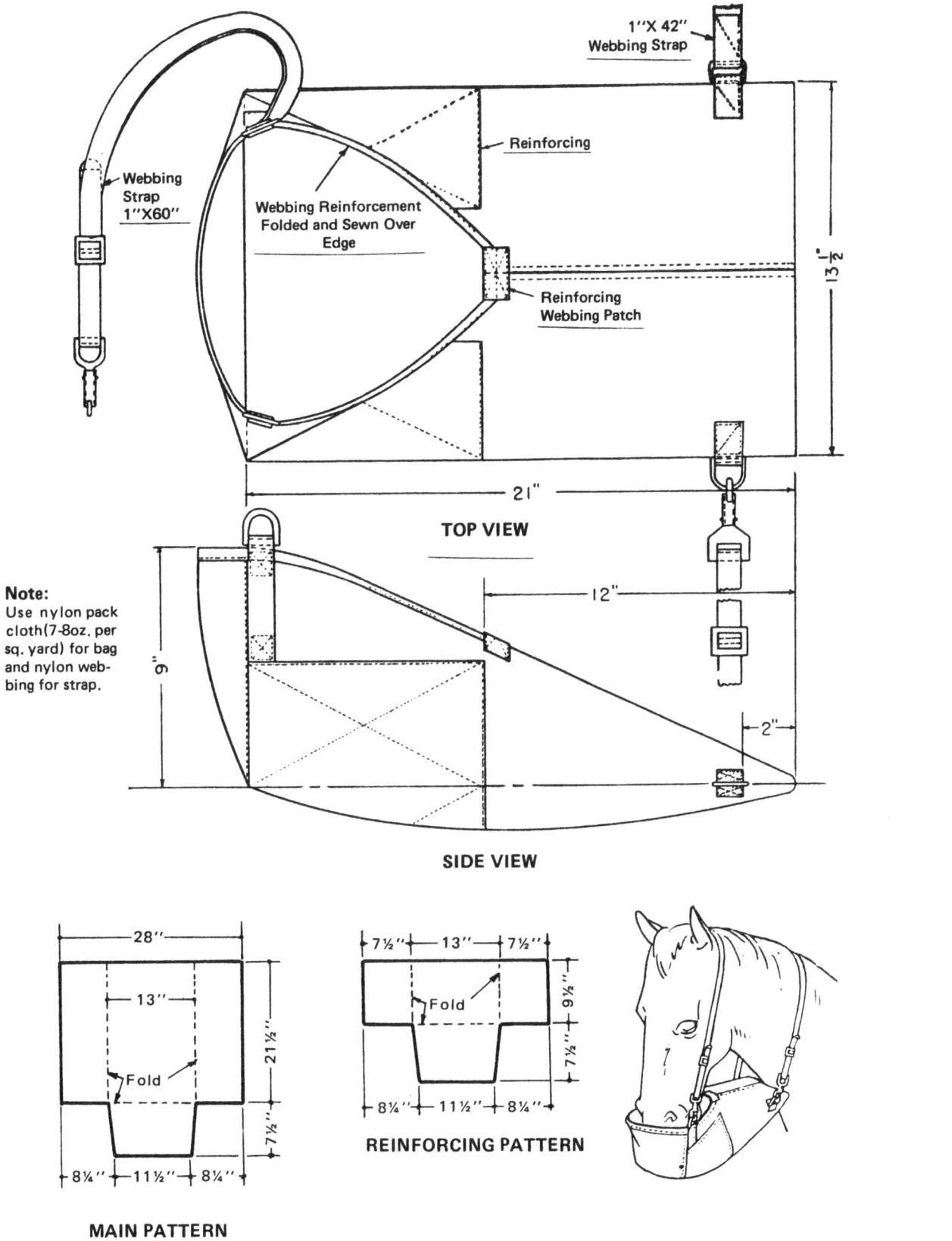

NOSE FEED BAG

APPENDIX D
Picket-pin

MATERIALS LIST					
NO	PART NAME	REQD	MATERIAL DESCRIPTION	SHEET
1	ROD	1	1/2 DIA 1020 STEEL ROD	
2	AUGER	1	1/8 THICK X 2 1/2 1008 HR STRIP OR 1/2 ID X 2 1/2 FENDER WASHER	

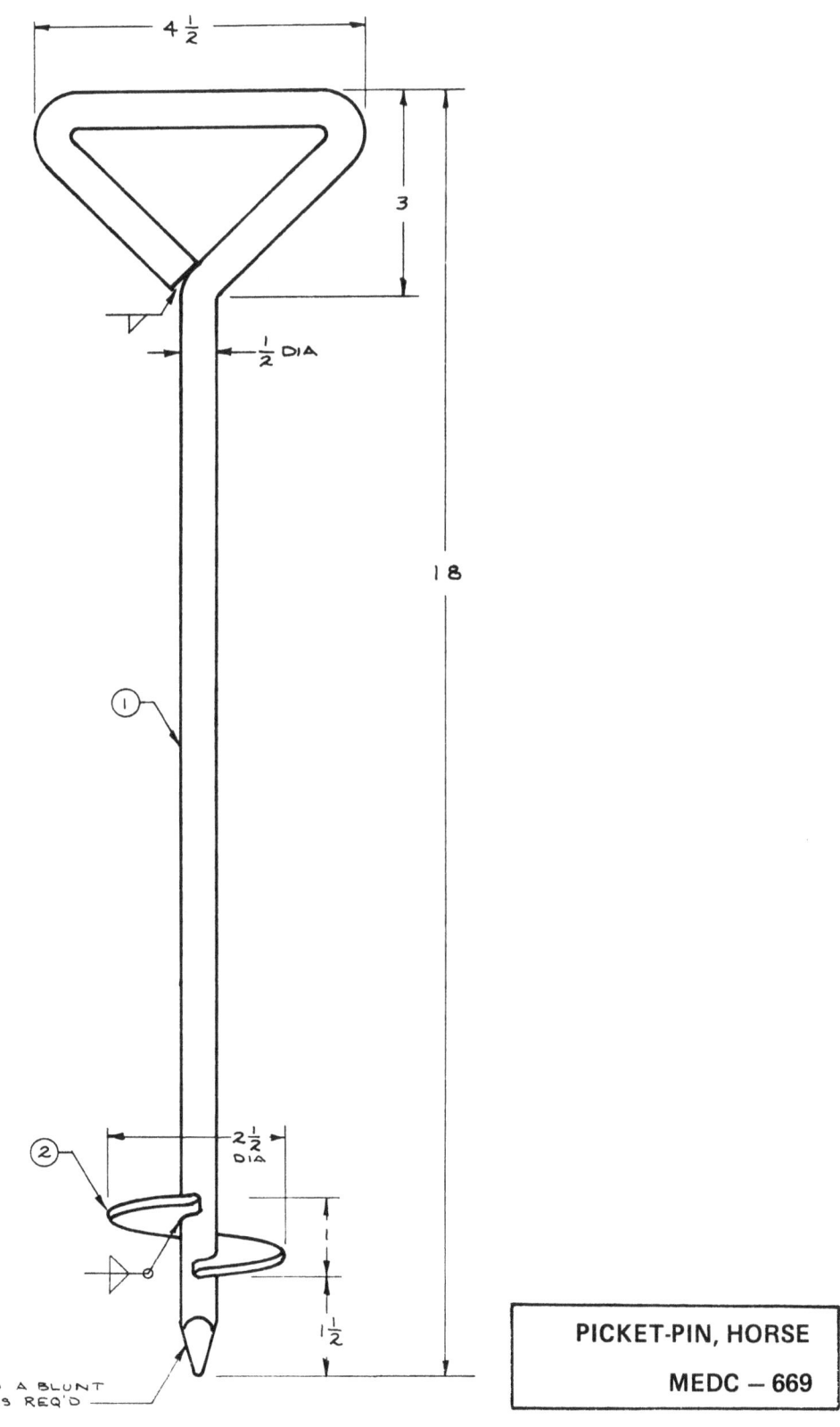

PICKET-PIN, HORSE

MEDC – 669

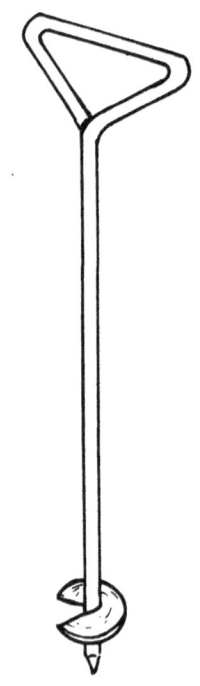

TURN STAKE INTO GROUND
BY HAND OR WITH A STICK
THRU HANDLE.

SWIVEL SNAP   PEAR LINK   LINK

USE ONE OF THE ABOVE METHODS TO PICKET STOCK
TO STAKE. PEAR LINK CAN BE TURNED ON TO STAKE
BEFORE INSERTING IN GROUND. LINK TYPE MUST
BE ASSEMBLED ON ROD BEFORE AUGER IS ATTACHED.

APPENDIX E
Tree Saver Strap

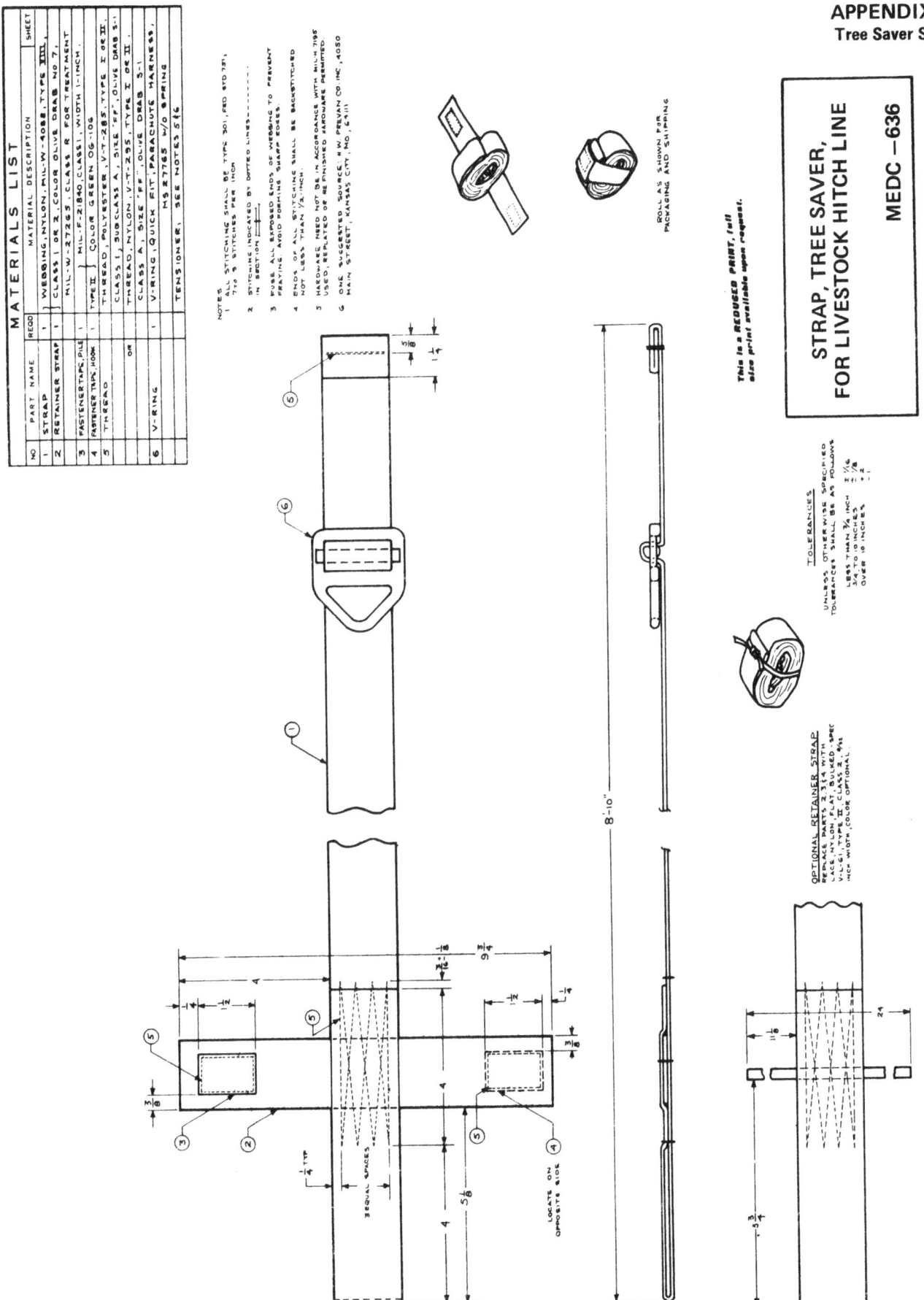

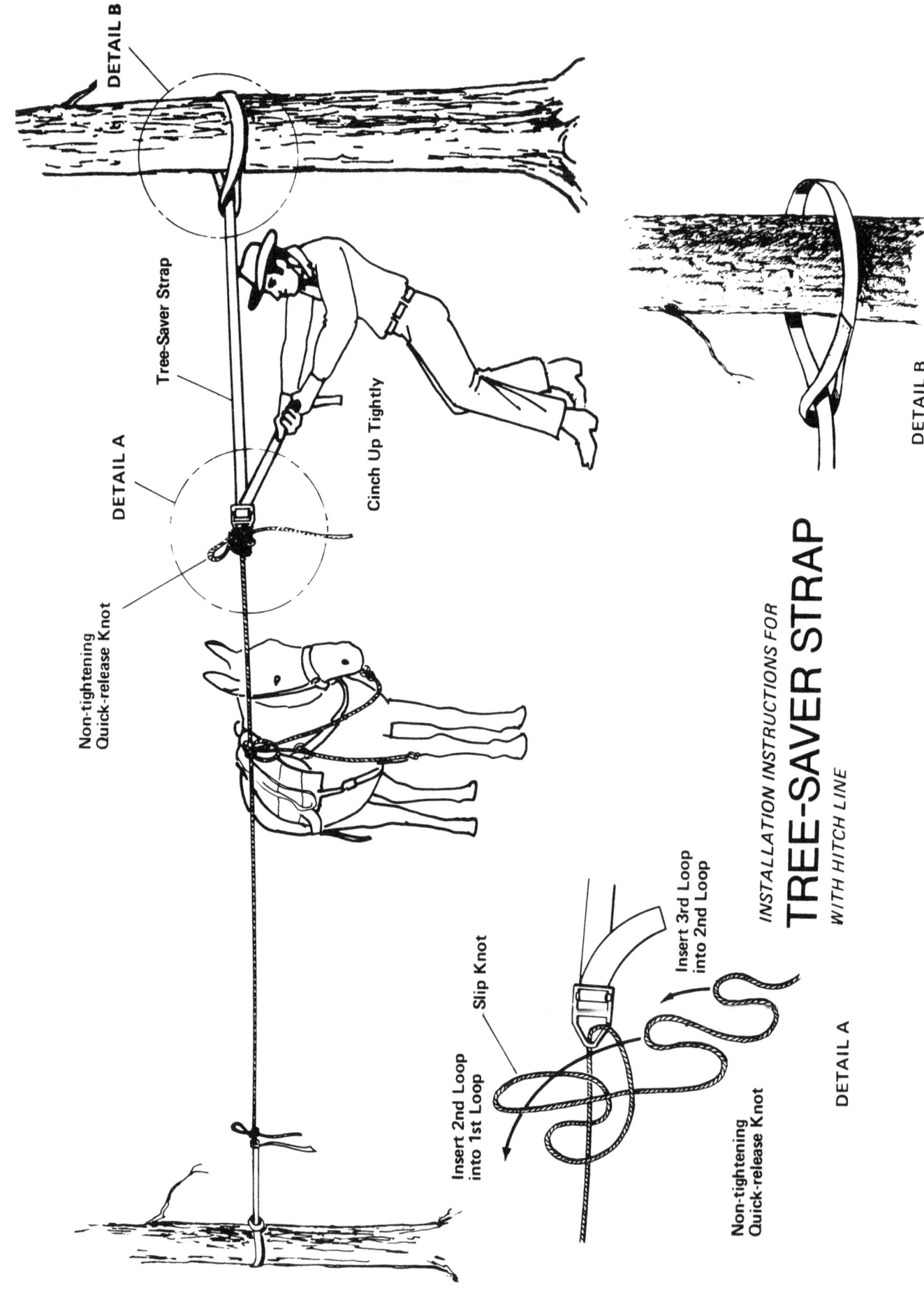

www.ingramcontent.com/pod-product-compliance
Lightning Source LLC
LaVergne TN
LVHW061317060426
835507LV00019B/2202